Undercover Diabetes Health Agents!

written by
Michelle Lombardo, D.C.

illustrated by
M.R. Herron

A special thanks to the following for their review and expertise:

Alice Carroll, LDN. RD and Nancy Laird,
Consultants, Louisiana Department of Education

Andrew Muir, M.D.
Chief, Pediatric Endocrinology, Medical College of Georgia

Beth Reames, PhD, LDN, RD,
Professor and Extension Specialist (Nutrition and Health), LSU AgCenter

WELLNESS

INCORPORATED

Hi there! For those of you who don't know me, I'm Hardy Heart, leader of The OrganWise Guys Club. You may be wondering what I'm dong in this trench coat. Well, this week we have uncovered a serious health issue! It is a health problem that doctors call "diabetes." You may have heard the name, but as an undercover health agent I've discovered most people have no idea what it is!

That's where we come in ...the Undercover Diabetes Health Agents. Our mission is to help you, as well as one of our new agents, learn all about diabetes and what can be done to help prevent the most common type from happening to you. Do you know which OrganWise Guy should be concerned about helping kids stay healthy so they won't get diabetes when they get older? This is a tough question that is usually taught in medical school. Go ahead and take a guess which organ you think diabetes affects.

. . . It's that wild and crazy Peter Pancreas! And our mission, which we **decided** to accept, was to help turn Peter Pancreas into the lead Undercover Diabetes Health Agent! Talk about an *Impossible Mission*!

In order to handle this mission carefully, we brought Peter to the inside chambers (also known as our clubhouse!). Once we got him to settle down (he is an active little guy) Pepto began explaining to Peter how important the pancreas' role is in digestion.

Pepto explained . . .

"The digestion process begins in the mouth by chewing food.

After swallowing, the food travels down the esophagus and into the stomach. My job, as the stomach, is to make juices that continue to break down the food for the body to use.

The food then goes into the small intestines. Peter, this is the beginning of **one** of your jobs. The pancreas releases **enzymes** for digestion into the small intestines to help break the food down into even smaller pieces."

Peter, of course, thought he already had it figured out. He jumped up and shouted, "Okay, I've got it! Diabetes happens when I stop making digestive enzymes. That wasn't so difficult to understand. Now please give me my trench coat and let's get back to having fun!"

"Not so fast," Pepto said as he led Peter Pancreas back to his seat. "Making enzymes is just **one** of your jobs. You have another one further down the line in the digestive process. Let me continue, please."

"Once the food particles become very, very small, the food can then go through the walls of the small intestines and into blood vessels for the rest of the body to get the nutrients. As you know from being an OrganWise Guy, foods come in the form of proteins, fats and carbohydrates. What we want to talk about today are the carbohydrates.

Fruits, vegetables, grains, cereals, and sweets contain carbohydrates. These foods are broken down into simple sugars. Once these simple sugars are in the blood, they are ready to be delivered to all of the cells in your body. The key word here, Peter Pancreas, is **READY**! This is where your REALLY, REALLY important job comes in!" exclaimed Pepto.

"The pancreas' job is to make **insulin**. I like to think of insulin as a magic key that can open the lock at the gateway of each cell," said Pepto.

"Once the insulin keys are released into the blood, they unlock the gate so that the sugars can enter into the cells.

Cells are like factories and the sugar is similar to electricity. The cells need these sugars to keep everything going," said Pepto.

Peter Pancreas had quite a concerned look on his face. "Yikes, no wonder you've got me in the spotlight. My job really is important! If the cells don't get the sugar to run them, it could be a nightmare! So is that what diabetes is?"

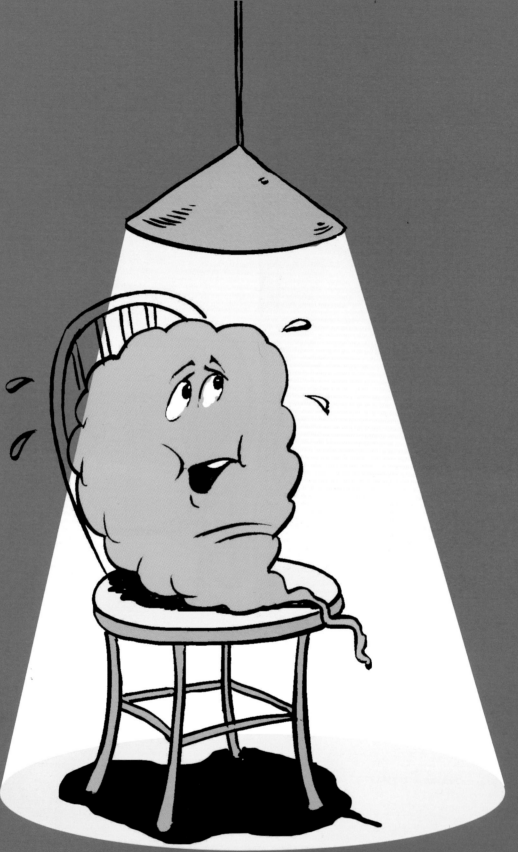

"Exactly! This is a serious thing," said Pepto. "Diabetes can happen in two ways. The first one is called Type 1 Diabetes. Type 1 Diabetes occurs when the body's immune system destroys the cells that make insulin. When this happens the pancreas just can't make insulin. There is nothing a person can do to prevent this type of diabetes.

Thankfully, these people can take insulin throughout the day, which is usually in the form of a shot. If you know of someone with Type 1 Diabetes, they can probably tell you what it takes to stay healthy and how careful they need to be about their food choices."

"The other form, which is what we want to talk about today, is called Type 2 Diabetes and is caused by the insulin keys not being able to work properly. The insulin keys and the lock on the gate just don't seem to match. Type 2 Diabetes may possibly be prevented or delayed by adopting a healthy lifestyle. In Type 2 Diabetes, the pancreas can still make the insulin; it is just not working correctly."

"So what kinds of healthy choices should people make?" Peter inquired.

"Glad you asked!" continued Pepto. "By making the choice to eat low-fat, high-fiber foods, exercise regularly and make water the beverage of choice, people can help to make sure their insulin keys work properly."

"For starters, too much fat in your diet can mean there is too much fat in your blood. This extra fat can get in the way of the insulin keys trying to do their job. Remember, their job is to open the gate so the sugars can enter the cells. If there is a lot of fat in the blood, it can get in the way of the insulin keys!" continued Pepto.

Solution #1 - Choose low-fat foods!

Exercising is another way to decrease the fat. Staying at a healthy weight is very important for helping the insulin keys to operate correctly. When you exercise, your muscles burn fat for energy. This includes walking, swimming, dancing, bike riding, skating and all types of physical activity that keep you moving! Exercising is a fun way to help maintain a healthy weight!

Solution #2 - Get plenty of exercise!

What more can be done to help with the process of carbohydrate digestion? What else will help things run smoothly for the insulin keys? Call on the *Fiber Guys* to help!

The type of carbohydrate you choose can make a big difference. This first cereal has 0 grams of fiber. Without fiber, carbohydrates are easily broken down into simple sugars, quickly go through the digestive system and flood into the blood. This causes very high levels of sugar in the blood all at once and can leave you hungry in a very short while.

Serving Size: 1 Cup
Fiber: 0 grams

Serving Size: 1 Cup
Fiber: 8 grams

Now let's look at a cereal choice that contains 8 grams of fiber. By having fiber mixed in with the carbohydrate it takes longer for the stomach to empty. For instance, a sugar goes out, a fiber goes out, a sugar goes out, a fiber goes out and so on! This keeps you full and satisfied for a longer period of time.

By adding fiber to your diet, the sugars are released more slowly into the blood. This allows the pancreas to pace itself and pump out insulin at a nice steady rate. This, of course, helps keep sugar levels in the blood more stable. So, the fiber guys are like little workers keeping things running smoothly throughout the whole process of sugar digestion.

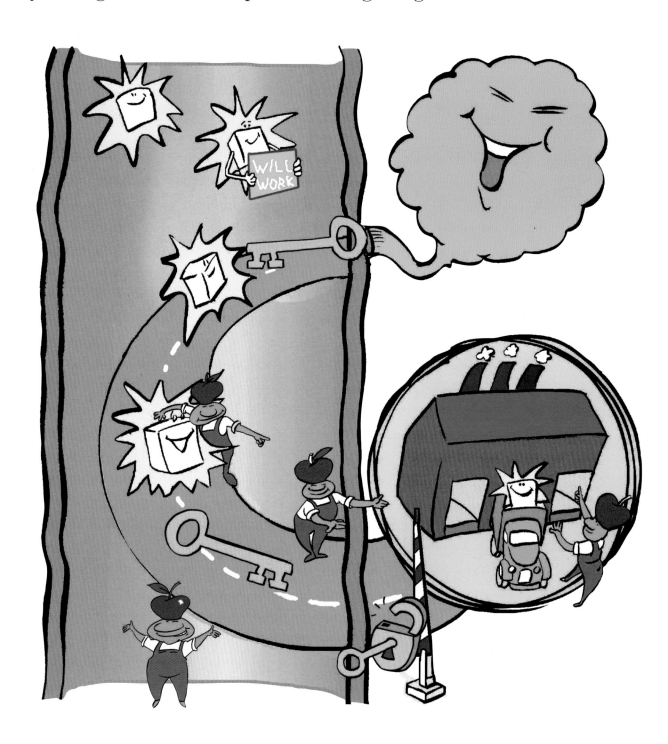

Solution #3 - Eat high-fiber foods!

Another way to help keep the sugar levels stable is to make water the beverage of choice. All of your organs need plenty of water to function properly. Water has zero calories and zero sugars. We OrganWise Guys like to think of water as giving us a nice, clean shower. Be sure to drink plenty of water everyday!

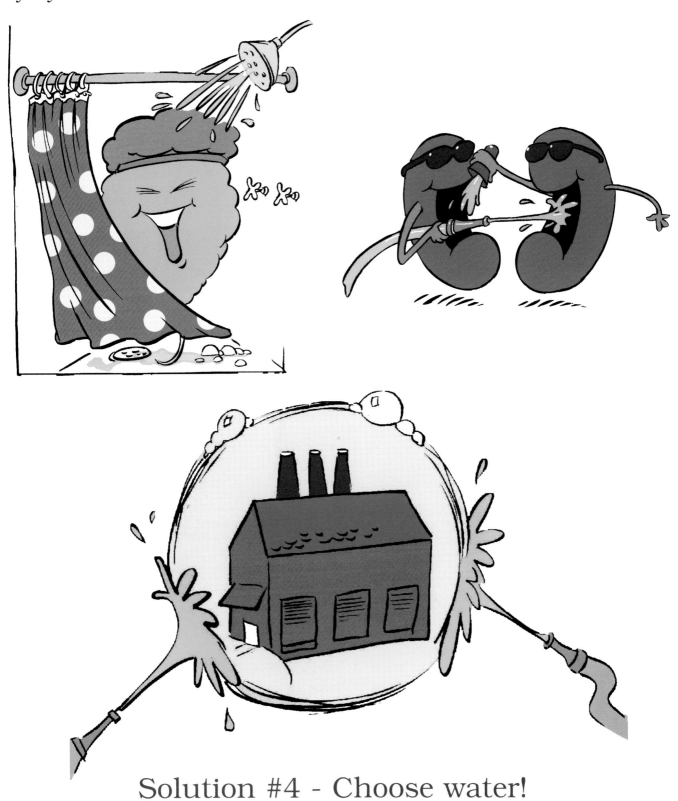

Solution #4 - Choose water!

"Now Peter," Pepto continued in a very serious tone, "there is one thing to be aware of when it comes to diabetes. One of the signs that a person may have diabetes is an uncontrollable thirst. This is more than just being thirsty on a hot day. It is when a person feels like he/she just cannot drink enough water! They are ALWAYS really, really thirsty, even at night when they should be asleep. If someone you know is like this, get them to a doctor immediately."

By now Peter Pancreas looked worn out. This was a lot of information to give a pancreas all at once. We could tell it was time to lighten things up a little for Peter. For those of you who know him, he is just a happy-go-lucky pancreas who loves to have fun. So Sir Rebrum has set up a game to teach him how easy it is to make healthy choices. It's time to play...The Meal is Right!

Peter won the chance to play *The Over-Under Game.* To win, he needs your help to successfully build a lunch that is...

Over 10 grams of fiber
and
Under 10 grams of fat!

Here are his options. Which would you choose?

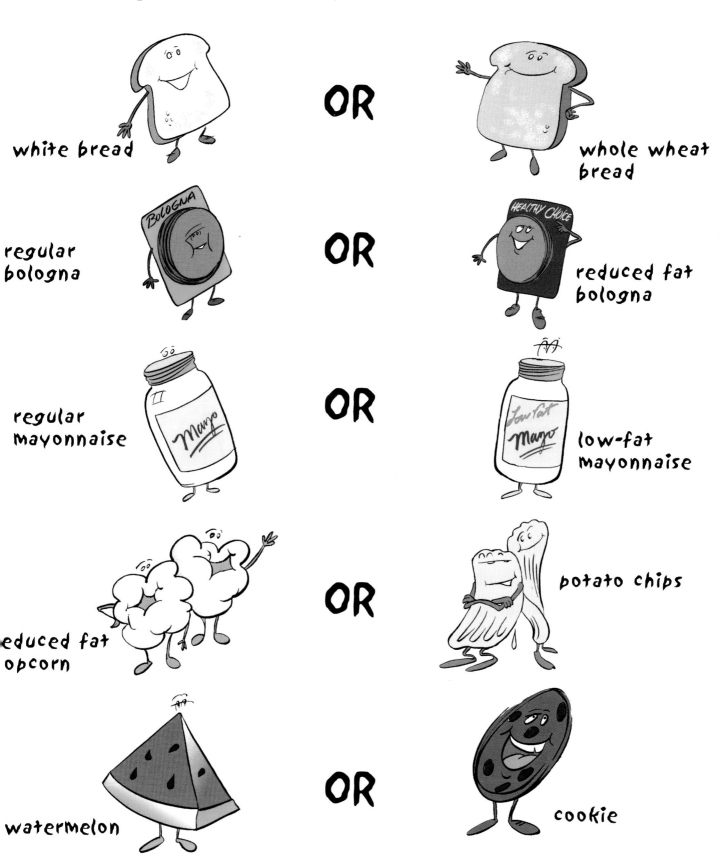

white bread   OR   whole wheat bread

regular bologna   OR   reduced fat bologna

regular mayonnaise   OR   low-fat mayonnaise

reduced fat popcorn   OR   potato chips

watermelon   OR   cookie

These are the items Peter chose with their fiber and fat counts.

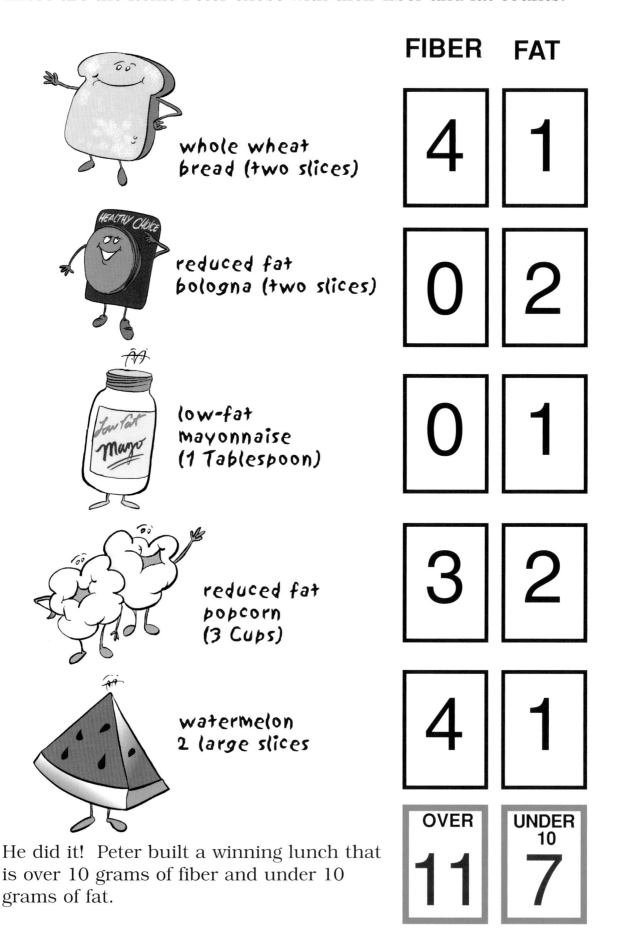

FIBER FAT

whole wheat
bread (two slices)
4 1

reduced fat
bologna (two slices)
0 2

low-fat
mayonnaise
(1 Tablespoon)
0 1

reduced fat
popcorn
(3 Cups)
3 2

watermelon
2 large slices
4 1

He did it! Peter built a winning lunch that
is over 10 grams of fiber and under 10
grams of fat.

OVER
11

UNDER
10
7

But before they award Peter his prize, let's take a look at how the numbers would have come out if he had picked the other foods!

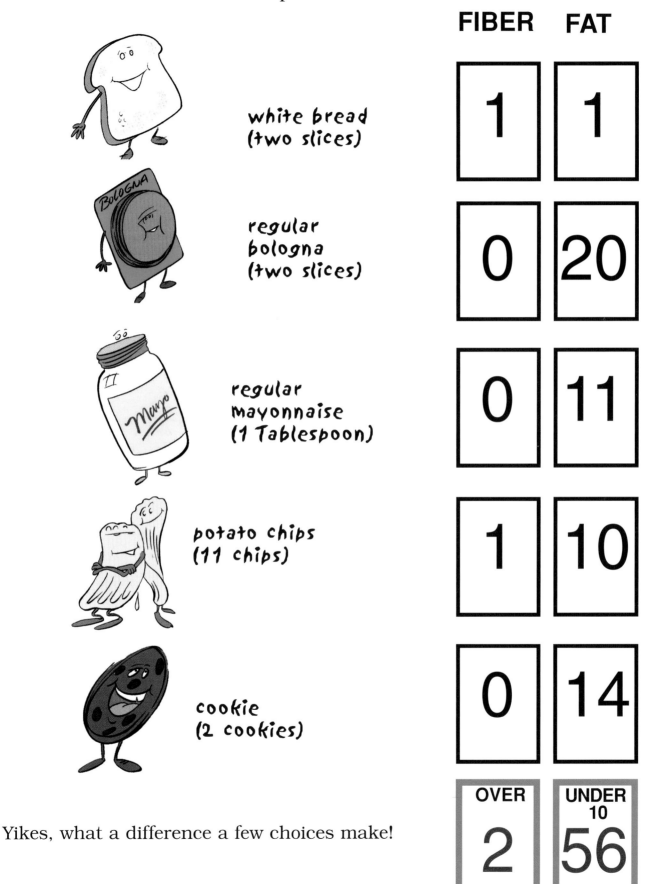

	FIBER	FAT
white bread (two slices)	1	1
regular bologna (two slices)	0	20
regular mayonnaise (1 Tablespoon)	0	11
potato chips (11 chips)	1	10
cookie (2 cookies)	0	14
	OVER 2	UNDER 10 56

Yikes, what a difference a few choices make!

It was now time to award our new Undercover Diabetes Health Agent his own official trench coat and spy magnifying glass for reading food labels. Although this was a stressful undercover operation for us, we are glad that Peter is the lead agent when it comes to helping teach others about diabetes and how healthy lifestyle choices can make a difference in possibly preventing Type 2 Diabetes! And don't forget, we are also counting on you to share this information with your family and friends. Make it your mission to be a messenger of good health!